Goa

CW00631994

Goalkeeping in Action

Peter Shilton

Stanley Paul
London   Melbourne   Auckland   Johannesburg

Stanley Paul & Co. Ltd

An imprint of Century Hutchinson Ltd

Brookmount House, 62–65 Chandos Place
Covent Garden, London WC2N 4NW

Century Hutchinson Australia (Pty) Ltd
PO Box 496, 16–22 Church Street, Hawthorn,
Melbourne, Victoria 3122

Century Hutchinson New Zealand Limited
191 Archers Road, PO Box 40–086, Glenfield,
Auckland 10

Century Hutchinson South Africa (Pty) Ltd
PO Box 337, Bergvlei 2012, South Africa

First published 1988

Set in Monophoto Times

Printed and bound in Great Britain by
Butler & Tanner Ltd, Frome and London

British Library Cataloguing in Publication Data
Shilton, Peter
　Goalkeeping in action.
　1. Soccer——Goalkeeping
　I. Title
　796.334′26　　GV943.9.G62
ISBN 0 09 171261 0

Frontispiece:
Marshalling the troops

Contents

Acknowledgements

The author and publishers would like to thank Dennis Coath for all his help in the preparation of this book. Also Roy Pell and Alec Daniels for all the specially taken photographs including the 'flicker' sequences. The match action photographs were provided by Colorsport and All-Sport.

Introduction

You've got to be daft to be a goalkeeper, they always tell me, but other players are often jealous of the most influential and important member of the team. I believe that you need greater all-round ability to play between the sticks than in any other position. A goalkeeper needs the nimbleness of an outfielder, the resilience of a rugby forward and the handling skills of a basketball player.

A goalie's apprenticeship is long and hard. Unlike players in other positions, he doesn't usually reach his peak until about 30 years old. That is the time when a keeper is the ideal mixture of experience and athleticism. It is also encouraging to know that a goalkeeper's career is quite often longer than an outfield player's. In goal, experience and positional sense can more than compensate for slowing reactions and advancing years. Pat Jennings of Northern Ireland and Italy's Dino Zoff both played in the final stages of the World Cup when they were past 40. That would be highly unlikely in any other position on the field.

For any youngster starting out in the Number 1 jersey, it's important to master the basic skills. Spectacular acrobatic dives are little use if you can't even catch the ball. If you don't position yourself correctly, or use your body to the greatest possible advantage, goalkeeping would be very hard work indeed. If you make a wonderful save and then throw the ball out to an opponent's feet, then all your efforts may be wasted.

It's always surprised me that specialised training has been a fairly recent innovation in our football. At one time keepers used to spend all their time working out with the rest of the squad. Now most clubs have specialised sessions for their goalkeepers, often under the guidance of former internationals like Gordon Banks and Alan Hodgkinson.

Neville Southall of Wales, Scotland's Jim Leighton and the great Pat Jennings are three top-class internationals of recent years who would be first-choice keepers for virtually any country in the world. In the England team we have established a tradition of long-serving goalkeepers with players like Gordon Banks, Ray Clemence and myself. But if high standards are to be maintained, we must teach up-and-coming players good habits to start with; natural flair can then develop.

I am well aware that there is a tradition in this country for players to turn to goalkeeping as a last resort. Sometimes youngsters cannot get a place on the field in their school or youth team so they have a go at goalkeeping. The position should never be an afterthought or filled by a stop-gap. What is the use of having a sound team if you have an apathetic goalkeeper who cannot catch a ball or stop a shot.

If you are a goalkeeper, then you are a humble member of one of sport's most exclusive clubs ... the players who wear that coveted Number 1 jersey. I am proud to have earned the record number of caps for an England keeper and sincerely believe that in goalkeeping standards Britain leads the way.

By reading this book, and studying the pictures, you will not achieve perfect goalkeeping overnight, but it could be your starting point in succeeding me in the England team.

I hope this guide will be a pointer in the right direction and help all aspiring goalies to learn the rudiments of the best trade in soccer.

Pat Jennings – one of Britain's greatest ever
international goalkeepers

Don't let your concentration lapse

Shot stopping

Body behind the Ball

Concentration

Whether you are in goal for England in a
World Cup final or playing in a Sunday
morning park game, shots can fly in
from any angle or distance. It doesn't
matter how much ability you have, if
you don't concentrate, you cannot do
the job properly. That applies to any
position, but particularly to goalkeeping. A local league player is just as likely
to surprise you with a snap shot as a top
international.

The most important fact to remember
about goalkeeping is that you have to
concentrate for the full 90 minutes of a
match, even though you're not involved
in play for much of the time. When the
action comes your way you have to be
ready to react. If your mind is wan-
dering you will fall down in your job as
the last line of defence.

If your side is dominating a match,
you could be reduced to the role of a
spectator for long periods of the game.
Sometimes you feel as though you're
never going to touch the ball. Suddenly
there's a surprise attack ... and you're
not prepared ... the opposition score
and, despite being in total command of
the game, your side is 1–0 down. In

Saving at Feet

Taking a Cross

Penalty Save

11

situations like this the goalkeeper has let his team mates down through lack of concentration.

Don't be caught out!

Anticipation

Anticipation can save a goalkeeper from wasting energy. What we really mean by anticipation is keeping one step ahead of the opposition. You almost need to develop a sixth sense to read players' minds and guess the direction in which a ball will travel. As few of us are likely to develop psychic powers, we can only improve our reading of the game by practice and experience. A vital split second gained by making the right movement may mean the difference between letting in a goal and making a miraculous save. To use an example, if a goalie decides that one of his own defenders might fail to cut out a cross, he can prepare for the eventuality before it happens, rather than leaving it too late.

Always change your position round the goal as the ball is moving. You should be altering your position as the ball moves from one player to another and not as someone is about to shoot at goal. When facing a shot you must be set and balanced. A goalkeeper mustn't wait for the action and then move into position. He must be at a point of readiness when one of the opposition strikes the ball.

12

Action stations

Anticipation is often a case of picking the right option. It can be a battle of wits between a goalkeeper and a striker. When a forward runs toward goal at an angle, the keeper should have the upper hand and leave the striker less goal to aim at. The forward has three options. First he may try to blast the ball past you, probably inside the near post. Second, if he is skilful, he might try to chip the ball into the top corner. Third is the possibility that he will pass to an opponent in a more favourable position. It is vital that an alert goalkeeper is prepared to combat every attacking ploy.

The more you study opposing forwards, the better you'll be able to read the game. Through experience

13

Left a bit – you should be constantly changing your position as the ball moves

you'll recognise what a player intends to do through his body movement and the way he shapes up. If you make the right decision, your opponents will become more and more frustrated.

Remember that anticipation will help

you to keep the other team in their place and keep your goal intact.

Agility

Some people seem to think that agility is a quality that only relates to the twists, turns and contortions of top Olympic gymnasts. That type of movement isn't essential for goalkeepers, but a degree of natural agility is a major asset. What

15

Elastic body movement

is needed is the ability to change direction and move quickly in a confined space. That requires elastic body movement and good co-ordination.

Goalies rely on agility more than anyone else on the field. It is a question of using the whole of your body to the best possible advantage to stop the ball going into the net. You have to move your body mass around quickly and easily.

16

In improving agility, foot movement is the key. Studying other sports can help this aspect of keeping. For instance, watch the way American footballers and rugby players suddenly change direction. Look at the way boxers maintain their balance and keep out of trouble by using deft footwork. Then concentrate on moving your feet quickly around the goal area.

Agility is generated by the combined

17

Heavens above! Agility is an important asset for a goalkeeper

actions of the feet and head. If they move quickly then your whole body shifts accordingly. Some goalkeepers fling their arms at a shot and hope their feet and head will follow. As a result they're losing all their spring. By flapping at the ball you're losing the power of your body.

Once again we can use the actions of

a boxer for comparison. If he throws a punch by sticking out his arm, he loses the impact his body weight would create. If he moves his head and feet, he transfers his body power into the punch.

Getting off the floor quickly is another way a keeper can demonstrate his agility and make vital saves. When you're on the deck don't use your arms

and knees to get up ... you shouldn't be found scrambling to your feet. The correct approach is to react like a rubber ball and bounce up by using your shoulders in a rocking movement. You can save crucial seconds by springing, and not staggering, to your feet.

Although weight training can be useful to increase muscle, let me suggest one simple routine to develop fitness, strength and speed. Get someone to throw the ball a few yards either side of you, switching from right to left. Collect the ball and return it instantly. That means as soon as you have saved to your right and returned the ball, you've got to dive to the left to repeat the exercise. The effect is that you'll be rapidly moving up and down and from side to side. The method can be varied by having one ball thrown into the air and another low to the ground. This means a switch from stretching to catch a high ball to plunging downwards to stop a low one.

You don't need to be able to perform triple somersaults and back flips to be a top goalkeeper, but flexibility or agility is an important part of the trade.

Body behind the ball

As with agility, feet and head movements are critical in getting your body behind the ball. Obviously I realise that this isn't always possible when a keeper makes an instinctive save. Sometimes a

20

'Swallow' it

goalie does well just to get a touch to the ball, but I would advise youngsters always to try to move their whole body and not just their arms.

You should be attempting to move in line with the shot, displaying the powers of anticipation that we discussed earlier.

21

Body behind the ball

If you get your body behind a shot and the ball slips, then all is not lost, as it will hit your body or legs.

Always try to get your body as far across as you possibly can towards the ball. Then if you have to push out your arms to reach it, you'll find you have more strength to hold the ball or push it away. If you don't move your body, you're likely to parry the ball weakly and present a simple chance to an opposing forward.

22

When catching a ball try to 'swallow' it up with your arms. Treat it as your possession. Pull the ball into your body. If a shot is hit with stunning force and you're supple and well balanced, then you should be able to get behind the ball and cushion the blow. You should be able to absorb a shot rather like a car's shock absorber deals with a bumpy road. If you're stiff when you take the ball, it is likely to bounce from your grasp.

23

Cushion the blow

A goalkeeper should move as though he's in water. He must be loose and relaxed and not tense and rigid. The ease of a good disco dancer is another example of the sort of suppleness that is required.

Getting your body behind the shot will give you more strength, as well as that all-important second line of defence should the ball slip through your grasp.

Penalties

Confidence in your own ability is the most important factor in stopping penalties. A penalty kick is usually a moment of high drama in a match and an interesting situation for a keeper.

The onus is always on the penalty taker to score. He is in a 'no-win' situation. If he scores then he's only carried out the task expected of him. Should he fail then he'll sense the disappointment of his team mates and may feel the wrath of the crowd.

In contrast to that, the goalie is in a 'glory to nothing' situation although sometimes a keeper can be made to look foolish when he dives one way and a miss hit trickles into the centre of the goal.

There are many different theories on stopping penalties. One of the most successful ideas was dreamed up by the former Ipswich keeper Paul Cooper. He used to stand nearer to one post and sway towards the other. In that way he tried to shut out one side of the goal completely, tempting the kicker to aim for the bigger target on the other side. From his position off centre, Paul would motion his arms towards the more inviting space. That was a clever psychological ploy to

tease the striker of the ball and make him think.

I always follow three guidelines in trying to outwit the penalty taker.

1 Try to dictate the terms.
2 Stand up as long as you can.
3 Read the kicker's run up.

If a striker runs up in an arc, look right

26

The penalty is a one against one competition with the odds stacked in favour of the kicker, so make sure the contest is conducted to your advantage. Don't be rushed, remember the longer a player waits to take the kick, the more likely he'll be affected by nerves. Study the spot and give the impression that you're

confident and in charge. The referee will not whistle until you're ready, but it's best to be settled and in position as the kicker is placing the ball.

If you stand up as long as you can you're keeping your adversary guessing about which direction you're likely to dive. If a goalkeeper moves too early, all he is doing is making up the penalty taker's mind about which side of the goal to place the ball.

By carefully assessing a striker's run up, you can often work out where he's going to put the ball. If a right-footed kicker runs up straight, I feel that the ball is most likely to go to my left. If he runs up in an arc, it's more likely to travel to my right. When a player takes an extra long charge up to the ball, it usually means he's going to blast it.

Don't be disappointed if you fail to stop a spot kick. If a player hits the ball hard and low inside the post you shouldn't be able to reach it. So you've got to play the odds and hope that by reading the kicker's approach, by keeping your options open and by standing up until the last possible moment, you've a chance of making a save.

There are few better feelings in football at any level than saving a penalty.

Hot shots

In over 20 years in the game, and after a record number of England caps for a

28

goalkeeper, I have been under fire from the hottest shots in football. And although any player is capable of hitting that unstoppable 30-yarder, top internationals can strike the ball more consistently with accuracy and power.

The South Americans have always had a reputation for amazing, swerving shots, but the greatest striker of the ball in recent years is a European, the French star Michel Platini. His repertoire is extraordinary. When he's running on to

Michel Platini – an effortless striker of the ball

the ball he hits it swiftly, with hardly any backlift of his foot, with the result that the ball reaches you a split second quicker than from other players. He also has the gift of hammering the ball with great power and little effort, which is very disconcerting for a keeper. Another weapon in the Platini armoury is his skill at bending the ball around the defence. Even when you think you have gauged the angle correctly, he swerves the ball

Platini could place the ball on a ten pence piece

30

past you. Platini is probably most celebrated for his free kicks; he disguises his shots so well that if you move a moment too early, he can take advantage.

In one international in Paris he shaped up as though he was going to hit the ball over the wall and I moved too early to try to make a save. That was my biggest mistake as he placed it exactly in the place where I had been standing.

'Hot shot' Lorimer

The hardest shots I have ever encountered in my career came from Peter Lorimer of Leeds United and Scotland. It often felt as though he had fired a ball out of a cannon.

Malcolm Macdonald also packed a powerful wallop. When he was involved in shooting practice with the England squad you had to be very wary. If Super-

Supermac gives it a crack

mac caught the ball properly your hands could sting for minutes afterwards.

Kevin Sheedy of Everton is one of the most accomplished strikers of the ball currently playing in Britain. The biggest compliment I can pay Kevin is that he is not unlike Platini with his expertise at free kicks. He can put the ball to either side of you, and even if he fires it straight

Sheedy shapes up

you still have to hold on to it. Everton are very adept at following up Sheedy free kicks to pick up any rebounds. One

34

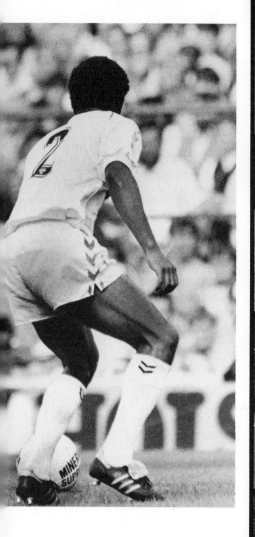

of the things that surprises me is that Kevin can generate a lot of pace with a chip over a defensive wall.

A Robson rocket on the way

Bryan Robson is underrated as a shooting star. He is another player who can strike with awesome power. When he tries a long shot it always seems to swerve, which makes it difficult to catch. Many players hit the ball hard and

Johnny Metgod – the Dutch master blaster

straight; Bryan is able to swing it like a fast bowler with a new ball.

Dutchman Johnny Metgod is another master blaster. I have never forgotten a free kick he scored for Nottingham Forest against West Ham. Even though his 30-yarder went into the centre of the goal just under the bar, it was travelling so fast that even Phil Parkes was unable to stop it.

Jimmy Case of Liverpool and Southampton is another who can launch the ball with rocket power. He's scored some memorable goals from outside the area.

37

Jimmy 'hard' Case

Glenn Hoddle – there's venom in his volleys

Probably the most artistic striker of the ball is Glenn Hoddle. He is very cunning and adroit at beating the goalkeeper's angle. Glenn is quick to spot a goalkeeper in the wrong position and defeat him with a cleverly placed chip. He is also one of the best volleyers I have ever seen, with the necessary technique both to keep the ball down and strike it with amazing speed.

Ian Rush and Gary Lineker are the

Gary Lineker salutes another England goal

two top goalscorers in my book; their records speak for themselves. Rush and Lineker are world-class strikers thanks to their pace and acceleration. They can deceive goalkeepers because they are able to delay their arrival in a danger area to the last moment, knowing that their speed will compensate for their late start. They both tend to 'ghost' in. The goalkeeper has difficulty spotting them coming.

41

Lineker on the way to his second hat-trick, against Poland

I have watched Gary at England sessions trying to make sure he is first to reach any ball played into the box. He often scores by making any sort of contact in the six-yard area. It might be a toe poke, a push from the knee or a deflection off any part of his body. That

makes it hard for a goalkeeper to antici-
pate the direction of the ball.

Rush and Lineker also use their
lightning speed and reflexes to arrive
late at the near post. Often the ball is
past you and into the net before you
realise what is happening.

43

Ian Rush's in where angels fear to tread

Great goals aren't the sole preserve of international stars like Rush, Lineker and Platini. Playing in goal for your local Sunday team you're quite likely to be faced with a lightning strike or a

swerving 30-yard shot into the top corner. That's all part of the trials and tribulations of the job. Always be prepared for the unexpected.

45

Crosses

Positioning

Positioning for crosses varies, but the basic rule is that you have to take up your stance in relation to how far the ball is away from the goal. If a ball is coming in from the edge of the box stand closer to the near post than if a cross is coming over from the touch line. The further the ball has to travel the more chance you have to leave your line. Try and attack crosses that you can reach comfortably. Don't come racing off your line for balls that you can leave to your defence, that only causes panic.

There is nothing I like better to see than a goalie coming for a long high cross and gathering the ball with time and assurance. You have to make a decision on which crosses to come for and which to leave to your defenders. On corner kicks make sure your defence is well positioned and your men are where you want them to be. Take up a position almost in the centre of the goal, just a yard nearer to the far post. Once again, your defenders should be well set so don't charge off your line for balls they can deal with.

Full stretch

Catching at the highest point

There are two fundamentals in the science of goalkeeping, catching at the highest point and narrowing the angle. A good understanding of these two facets of the game is the key to sound goalkeeping. Competence at these skills makes a goalie's life a lot easier. We look at narrowing the angle in the next section, but here I want to talk about catching at the highest point as this is

Reach for the sky – once committed, don't hold back

essential in dealing with crosses and corners.

The importance of taking the ball at the highest point is obvious: it allows the keeper to utilise his biggest asset over opposing forwards to maximum

48

advantage. That is, of course, the freedom to use his arms and hands when going for a ball in the air. At full stretch a keeper should always be able to gain possession over an opposing forward ... except perhaps if he's a seven-foot giant.

49

Any high ball into the penalty box from a cross or corner is a major threat. If the goalie is beaten to the ball or drops it, then the opposition will have a great chance to score. So the message that has to be hammered home is ... *keep your arms fully stretched when going for a high ball.* Many goalkeepers make the mistake of going for balls in the air with their arms bent so they don't make full use of their natural advantage. It's usually the result of slackness when a keeper is beaten to a high ball by an opposing striker. When a high cross comes over you should not allow it to drop to head height.

The only exception is when a centre is driven hard and fast at about head level; that can be a goalkeeper's nightmare as a striker can easily nip in front of you to score. The most important advice to remember is not to wait for the ball to come to you; someone is likely to beat you to it. If the ball is dropping to the near post, make the ground up as quickly as you can and, instead of letting the ball drop to your stomach, take it at head height. The earlier and higher you take the ball, the less likely you are to be beaten by the opposition.

Catching the ball at full stretch in a crowded goalmouth is when a goalkeeper is likely to face a physical challenge. When you come out for a cross, don't have one eye on the ball and the

50

other on the oncoming forwards. That will affect your concentration and make you likely to fumble. Keep both eyes firmly on the ball, jump confidently at full stretch and use your body power. Once you are committed to go for a high ball don't hold back.

A goalie can suffer a few knocks taking a high ball, but if you jump properly there should be no real problem.

Opposition strikers will do everything they can to put you off, so you must be prepared to give as good as you get. Using the correct technique you should be able to shrug off most challenges. If you are timid and apprehensive, the opposition will exploit that weakness.

Cutting out the low ball

The sneak low ball to the near post is what a goalkeeper dreads most. Players will vary their passes into the box and you should not just be looking for the high looping cross. Centres can be driven in at waist height or along the floor. On short, low crosses, try to attack the ball before it goes past the near post. That is not always possible, but do attempt to reach the ball and get your body behind it as we have discussed.

Never move too early and guess where a cross might go. If you move out before a ball is played in, a miss-hit cross can skid along the ground and creep inside the near post. Make sure you keep

51

your arms above waist high when going for crosses. You need to be able to lift your arms quickly to reach the ball.

Punching

Punching is one art that is rarely mastered by goalkeepers. It is an aspect of the trade that requires hours of practice to perfect. You need to gain height and distance when you punch the ball. Whenever possible you should try to

Right: The right jab
Below: Another knockout punch

52

53

make a catch, but there is nothing worse than seeing a goalie trying to hold on to the ball at full stretch when under pressure and dropping it. He would have been better advised to punch it to safety in the first place.

You have to know when to punch and when to catch. If you are confident about your punching you can come out for more crosses, with the knowledge that if you cannot gather the ball cleanly, you can punch it 20 yards or more.

There is a similarity with snooker as the angle the ball is coming from dictates which direction a punch is going. This means if the ball is dropping short at the near post, you punch it back in the direction from which it came. A ball landing in the centre of the goal from the midfield should be punched down the centre of the pitch.

The punching action is important. Some goalies have a tendency to swing at the ball in the way a boxer throws a right or left hook. That means the arm is travelling too far, leaving a wider margin for error. Using a wild swing you may not be able to get your arm up to the ball in time, and with a swinging action it is difficult to make good contact. If you 'throw a haymaker' at the ball it could land anywhere, probably at the feet of an opposing forward! In order to punch well, you must move into a cross with your arm held high and use a quick jab which travels a short distance to impart power on the ball. That cuts down the risk of a mistake caused by a wild, unbalanced swing.

Just as strikers practise hitting the ball with their weaker foot, so goalkeepers need to work on punching with their weaker arm. It is always an advantage to be able to punch with both fists. Look how it has benefited Marvin Hagler and Mike Tyson!

Top crossers

It's very difficult to pick out just a few good crossers of the ball. I've met many great players in my 20 years who excel at this aspect of the game. In the same way that a local league or park player can surprise a goalkeeper with a long shot, he's also just as capable as a top professional of providing a telling cross on occasions.

The first player I admired for his ability to centre the ball was Terry Paine who played for Southampton and England. Few players could beat Terry in his accuracy at placing the ball. He could drop it on the proverbial sixpence, setting up chances for strikers and making life hard for a goalie.

My England colleague, John Barnes of Liverpool, is a brilliant crosser of the ball. He can deceive a goalkeeper by putting pace and bend on the ball. John plays in the type of centres that tease and tantalise a keeper. The more you come out of your goal, the further the

55

Above: John Barnes showing South American style in Chile

Left: A Paine in the neck for goalies and Bobby Moore

ball seems to swing away from you. When pace is added to swing, it makes it difficult for a goalkeeper to commit himself.

Two players I mentioned in the section on hot shots are also excellent at playing the ball into the penalty area. Both Kevin Sheedy and Glenn Hoddle can match their excellent shooting with top-quality passes and centres. Although they are both essentially midfield players, Kevin and Glenn can find space on the flanks, Glenn usually cen-

57

The Sheedy right foot ready to deliver

Glenn Hoddle – an artist at work

tering from the right and Kevin from his position on the left-hand side. Both players can chip the ball effortlessly into the box, usually finding the chosen target.

Surprisingly one of the best foreign exponents at crossing and centering that I have seen, played most of his club and international football at full back. German defender Manny Kaltz used to make overlapping runs and centre the ball with a technique similar to John Barnes. He proved that you didn't have to be a winger or midfield player to be an expert crosser of the ball. Unexpected quality centres from full backs can add to a goalkeeper's problems in commanding the penalty area.

Manny Kaltz – a defender with a winger's touch

John Robertson – the best crosser of the ball I've seen

Perhaps the best crosser of the ball that I have witnessed was my old Nottingham Forest colleague and former Scotland international John Robertson. 'Robbo' played with me in the famous Forest side built by Brian Clough and Peter Taylor that won the Championship and League Cup 'double'.

Robertson could hit a moving or dead ball with unerring accuracy. It was the way he varied his delivery of the ball that made him an international winger. Sometimes he'd lob the ball, at other times he'd clip it, bend it or drive it low and hard. His telling centres often frustrated defences and led to goals. When a goalkeeper is dealing with a man who can centre like John Robertson he has to cater for every possibility.

Coming off your line

Dominating the box

The six-yard box is your sanctuary, but a goalkeeper should also be able to command the penalty area. That is his territory.

There's an old maxim that every ball in the six-yard box should be your property. That's still good advice for a youngster, but a good goalkeeper can dominate the whole penalty area. As I mentioned in the section about crosses, he must be able to come off his line and catch or punch safely. It is reassuring for a defence when the keeper has the ability to take the ball as far out as the penalty spot. That kind of domination takes pressure off the other defenders and they can readjust their positions around the keeper.

You can only have one boss in the penalty area and that must be the goalie. If he's confident in the box then that attitude will rub off on the players around him.

Narrowing the angle

Now we come to our second 'science' – narrowing the angle. As with catching at the highest point, mastery of this technique makes a goalkeeper's life a lot easier.

62

They shall not pass

Narrowing the angle simply means making life difficult for an opposing player by making the goal appear smaller (see above). What the keeper is trying to do is leave the striker with as little goal as possible to aim at. If a shot from the edge of the area is placed just inside the post and the keeper is rooted to his line, he'll have little chance of making a save. If he advances four or five yards, he'll only need to dive about half the distance to make a save. That is what we mean by narrowing the angle.

If a player breaks through and you've started from your goal line to meet him, you will probably be between the six-yard box and the penalty spot when he shoots, giving him a large target area. Now suppose you are on the six-yard line as you start to advance, then you'll confront your opponent between the

63

penalty spot and the edge of the penalty area. As a result he won't have much of the goal to shoot at as you will have narrowed the angle efficiently.

A simple home experiment will teach you the importance of cutting down the striker's target. Using a table football set, shine a torch into the goal from just outside the penalty box. Then put a model footballer, or a similar object, in between the goal and the torch. Imagine that the torch is the onrushing forward and the model is the goalie. The closer you move the model towards the torch, the bigger the shadow will be on the goal – an illuminating way to demonstrate how narrowing the angle reduces a forward's sight of goal. The shadow is the area of the goal blocked by the keeper's body, the light parts to the sides are what is left for the forward to aim at.

When a goalkeeper has to narrow the angle it is one of the most crucial situations he faces in the game. It's the nearest he gets to a 'duel' with another player and, as when facing a penalty, the dice are loaded in favour of the kicker of the ball. A keeper usually faces this kind of situation when he has to deal with an onrushing forward who's got clear of the defence. It is in these situations that ace goalscorers like Ian Rush and Gary Lineker excel. A goalie has to think and act quickly. The first point to remember as you come forward is to stand up and do not commit yourself too early.

64

I'd better explain what I mean by 'standing up'. I've often seen goalkeepers leave their line to confront opponents and stand straight like a guardsman. As a result they can easily be beaten by a ball that goes under or just past them.

With an upright body, they cannot get down to the ball. The correct stance as you come out is to adopt a slight crouch with your shoulders bent and hands and arms low as in the photograph on page 63. You must be loose and relaxed and ready to react quickly.

A goalkeeper must win the duel by making the oncoming player beat him. As with any shot stopping situation, don't make the opposing player's mind up for him by diving to one side too soon, inviting him to place the ball to the other side. Similarly don't dive at the player's feet too early. That will give him a chance to dribble around you or chip the ball over your body. You've got to come out and stand up until the last possible moment.

When someone breaks clear, use those powers of anticipation. Don't advance from your line like a sprinter off his starting blocks. That makes it difficult for you to change direction and easy for a player to run around you. By tearing out at full speed you don't have enough control of your movements. It is also important to note that if you leave your line too early, you're wide

65

open to a chip shot or lob over your head. There is nothing worse than straining to reach the ball as it sails over you and into the net. However, if you are too slow out of your goalmouth, you leave that wider target either side of your body; you must be just far enough from your line to cut down the angle, reduce the striker's options and catch him in two minds.

By coming to meet an opponent at the right pace you'll force him to think

Platini makes a swallow dive after losing a duel

rather than act. As you're relaxed, balanced and not charging out, he is going to find it difficult to dribble past you without you plunging at his feet. He's not going to be very confident of knocking it past you either, as he can see very little of the goal and he's got precious little room to chip it over you. Well, that's the theory anyway!

One fact to take into consideration is your height. If you are on the small side for a goalkeeper, you've got to be more

wary of the chip over your head. If you are tall then you have the option of coming out a little earlier. A big goalie should remember to crouch a little lower when coming out as he's going to have a harder job getting down to a low ball. That proves that it is not always an advantage to be a giant goalkeeper.

Courage

The old saying that you have to be daft to be a goalie came about because it is the position in the game where you're forced to take most risks. Risks can either lead to mistakes or injury. At the top level a goalkeeper has to be brave. If he had all the skill and technique in the world, he'd never become a professional without courage. In challenging for a ball in the air, or in diving at players' feet he is often putting himself at risk.

The classic situation is when a large striker is coming towards you at pace. You have got to show a certain amount of courage to dive at his feet. But don't flinch or hesitate, that's how you're most likely to get hurt.

I've often heard it said that you can teach players all sorts of skills but you can't coach them to be courageous. That's a quality you're born with. This is not entirely true as some players become braver as they get older and more experienced. The important fact to remember in these situations is that the better your technique the less likelihood

68

Don't hesitate

there is of you being hurt.

Going for the ball at an opposing player's feet is a bit like making a rugby tackle, but in this instance your target is the ball and not the man. Watching a top-class wing forward or centre in rugby make a tackle will give you a few ideas. The method for a goalie dealing with an onrushing forward in a one against one confrontation is to go in for the ball with your hands first and make sure your head is going in behind. If you go for the ball and try to hold your head back you're likely to take a knock in the face or a bang on the head. So make sure you are compact when you go for the ball, with your head behind your hands; you can then use the whole weight of your body.

Above:
Lineker scores again as the Polish keeper goes in feet first

Below:
Don't take your eyes off the ball

It's when you see goalies going in feet first, or trying to hold their heads back, that you know they lack courage and are risking injury. When you go for the ball be determined that you're going to get there first. If you go in hard to win the ball you're less likely to be injured than if you flinch or shy away.

You must also ignore the onrushing player completely and concentrate on the ball. Don't take your eyes off the ball to watch the player. If a goalkeeper has courage allied with good technique, then he'll have a good chance of progressing in the game.

Reputations

I've often read newspaper reports which have said that a striker put clear of the defence muffed the chance because he looked up and saw me in goal. Once or twice on radio and television I've heard a commentator remark that a player hesitated because he realised he had to get the ball past Peter Shilton.

Those sort of comments are very flattering, but also utter nonsense. I suppose on the odd occasion a player may be daunted by the thought of beating Peter Shilton, Neville Southall or Jim Leighton, but it's unlikely in professional soccer. Do you imagine that strikers like Ian Rush or Gary Lineker pause for a second and fret about the goalkeeper they have to beat? I'm certain that opposing players never even

72

consider who's in goal when they're presented with a chance to score.

It's probably more likely that a striker confronted with a top goalie is going to be even more determined. He'll take extra credit for putting one past an international keeper.

If you turn the situation around, a goalkeeper shouldn't be in awe of Ian Rush or Gary Lineker. He's just got to concentrate on stopping the ball. So generally the notion that players with a scoring opportunity freeze when they come up against Peter Shilton is a load of rubbish. Reputations count for nothing. The only way you'll put pressure on opponents and stop shots is through superior technique, mixed with a little good fortune.

73

Organising the defence

Marshalling the troops

A goalkeeper has to be a dominant figure on the field in order to organise the players in front of him. That task becomes easier with experience, as a goalie acquires a better knowledge of the game.

Organisation of those in front of you is what I'd call my first line of defence. It's of vital importance. If the defence is organised and players are doing the right things, it makes it a lot easier for a goalkeeper to take up the correct position. When you're in goal and the players in front of you are all at sixes and sevens, you may find yourself taking up positions you don't want to just to cover for inadequate defenders. It helps a keeper to read the game a lot easier if there's a semblance of order in front of him.

In successful teams the defence is usually well marshalled and the goalie looks confident. If a defence is struggling, this has an adverse effect on the goalkeeper. He can't rely on his defenders and doesn't know where they are. As a result he may be caught flat footed in certain situations. No matter how badly the players in front of him are performing, people nearly always point the finger at the man in the jersey when the ball goes into the net.

Defenders in the wrong position can cause as many problems as a shot or a header. If someone doesn't make a tackle at the right moment, that can also make a goalkeeper's life more difficult.

It's the goalkeeper's task to place his defenders where he wants them in order to deal with set-piece situations. A free kick just outside the box is the classic example. If the goalie doesn't set up a defensive wall, then the opposition will have a straight shot at goal. So he has to use some of his team mates as a barrier to block out, or obscure, part of the goal; this reduces the kicker's target area. The keeper can then cover the remainder of the goal himself. The man between the posts must know exactly how he wants his defensive wall to line up and be positive with his instructions. The wall is usually made up of four or five players, but it can be as many as eight or as little as two, depending on the position of the free kick. The keeper covers one side of the goal and the players obliterate the rest by standing ten yards from the kicker. The theory is simple enough ... the kicker has to shoot at the side the goalie is placed to avoid the wall; the save should be straightforward!

Earlier I talked about the dead-ball skills of players like Michel Platini and

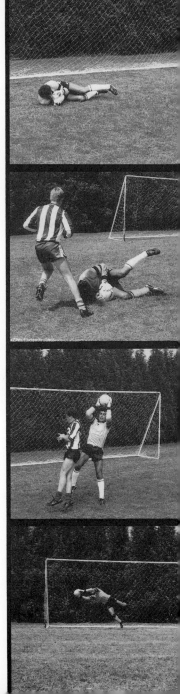

A solid wall

A yawning gap

79

Organising my first line of defence

Kevin Sheedy. More and more players have developed an ability to swerve the ball around a defensive wall or dip it over the barrier and just under the bar. I have seen this type of free kick from pub teams and Sunday league players, so beware!

If you plan your strategy correctly it should still be very difficult for a free kick to beat you from outside the box. The cardinal sin is to organise your wall and leave a small gap at the far end. Your defenders must blot out the kicker's view of the far post. Don't leave him a gap inside the post to aim at.

Shouting

Just because a goalkeeper does a lot of shouting it doesn't mean that he's a loudmouth. It should signal the fact that he is dominant and knows his job. Good, positive, shouting goes hand in hand with organising the defence. You have to make your presence felt and your voice heard. That's because a goalie is in the unique position of being able to see the whole field of play.

By shouting I don't mean bawling insults at the opposition or abusing your own defenders if they make a mistake. That is completely unnecessary and will be no help to the cause. Good shouting is a very constructive part of the goalie's game.

I always find that team mates like a keeper to be dominant and want to know what he's thinking. The goalkeeper provides what I term 'the eyes in the backs of other players' heads'. He can see everything planned out in front of him and can alert his colleagues to moments of danger.

Let me give you a few examples. A defender cannot see everything going on around him, but a keeper normally can. So he can let the player know if a striker has sneaked in behind him. He can shout to a full back to make a tackle on a

81

winger because he can see there's someone covering behind. When a forward's coming on to the defending centre half's blind side, he can instruct him to get the ball up the pitch quickly.

A shout from a goalkeeper should be positive. It should let those around him know exactly what he's going to do. Cries like 'leave it, John' and 'keeper's ball' leave no one in any doubt as to the goalie's intentions. In this way he will command the respect of his defence. Despite his dominance in the box, the keeper shouldn't be the only one giving out instructions. Defenders should also be making useful calls. For instance, when there's no challenge from an opposing forward, a defender may shout 'time' or 'catch it' to help out his keeper.

Providing 'the eyes in the backs of other players' heads'

When you're concentrating on the game by directing defenders and giving instructions in the box you're giving the team the feeling that you don't want to be beaten. If the keeper is not making himself heard, defenders won't be on their toes and it is then mistakes will happen.

Many people have observed that I shout more than most during the course of a match. To be good at anything you've got to be totally involved and dedicated to the job in hand. I shout at the players in front of me for several different reasons.

1 To tell them about a potential danger of which they are not yet aware.
2 To make sure they're marking their man properly.
3 To tell them about an opportunity to pass the ball that they cannot see.
4 To encourage them and help to keep up their enthusiasm.
5 And finally, and occasionally, to tell players off when they make a bad mistake or are being too casual.

Remember that shouting is mainly a constructive weapon for guiding your side and keeping each other informed. Shouting on the pitch provides essential communication for good team work.

Distribution

Creating moves

Distribution is the most undervalued part of the goalie's game. It's a skill that's often sadly neglected. The extra dimension a goalkeeper can add to a team with his creative work is under-estimated.

The main purposes of the Number 1 man in the side are to stop the ball going into the net and to gain possession. They must be top priority, but what is the use of making a fantastic save and then giving the ball straight back to the opposition to launch another attack? A goal-keeper should complete his job by making the stop and distributing the ball to a team mate.

In his own way a keeper can act as a playmaker, initiating moves from the penalty area and starting his side's attacks. Quite often a good throw or kick can lead to a goal. By using the ball sensibly to help your team keep possession, a goalie can take a lot of pressure off his colleagues.

Throwing

Now we move on to one of my pet hobby horses ... throwing. If the importance of distribution is neglected by

84

Ready to start a move

goalies, then throwing the ball is becoming a forgotten art.

I still feel that throwing is the best way for a keeper to start a move. It gives him the chance to transfer the ball swiftly, which can catch the opposition unawares. But you must not throw to players who are marked or likely to be easily dispossessed. Get rid of the ball to an outfield player who is in space. Speed is the essence: the shorter the time the ball takes to reach the intended player, the less chance an opponent has

85

of getting in a tackle. It also gives the receiver more time to get the ball under control.

When I first started out, Chelsea goalkeeper Peter Bonetti was a master at throwing the ball. He could reach the halfway line by hurling it, on a low trajectory, to his forward's feet. That was a great ploy for starting attacks.

The game now is played at such a fast pace that teams are preventing goalkeepers throwing out. I blame modern coaches for that. I would like to see

Quick roll out

more throwing, but now, as soon as a keeper has the ball in his hands, the teams push out en masse to the halfway line. I would like to see players spreading out to give their keeper more options for throwing the ball.

There are three basic styles used by goalkeepers. First there's the roll throw. This is a simple underarm roll out to a nearby, unmarked player, who is usually a defender no more than 20 yards away. The ball should be moved quickly so he has plenty of time to control it and set

Quick overarm clearance

an attack in motion. As with all throws, the goalkeeper should make sure team mates are aware of his intentions. The action should be accompanied by a warning shout.

Second there's the quick overarm clearance to midfield, the ball should be propelled hard and low to reduce the time the opposition have to make a challenge.

The third method is the long throw. You can fling the ball with an overarm

A bowling action to rival Botham

action nearly as far as a kick, but with a great deal more accuracy. Few keepers use this technique as they prefer to kick, but with practice you should be able to reach the halfway line and the feet and heads of your forwards. If you practise these three methods of throwing it will pay dividends.

The overarm action is not unlike that of a top-class bowler in cricket; watch the way they use their body power, shoulders and arms to propel the ball.

89

This style is particularly relevant to the low, flat throw to midfield.

Finally, of course, throwing the ball out quickly means that the game is kept in motion, thus adding to the general excitement.

Kicking

Now we move on to one of the most basic skills in the game ... kicking. Don't forget that a goalie can score with a kick. It's one of the rarest and usually one of the most comical events in the game. I'm fortunate enough to be one of the select band of goalscoring goalkeepers. Pat Jennings and Steve Ogrizovic are two other members of this exclusive club. I've heard plenty of stories of keepers getting on the score sheet in park and pub football, but that is often on pitches that are of minimum length.

Funnily enough I managed my one and only goal for Leicester City at Southampton many years ago. It's a moment I'll never forget. Everything was in favour of a long carry. It was downhill and the wind was at my back. We were leading 4–1 at the time when I hammered a volley kick as hard as I could downfield. The ball sailed into the Southampton half, skidded on the wet surface and went over the home keeper Campbell Forsyth and into the net to complete a 5–1 victory. Although I was delighted to score, it's not something you like to do to a fellow member of the goalkeeper's union. I know how embarrassed I would feel if it happened to me.

Goalkeepers, like any other players, have one stronger foot and like to use it for most kicks. As with outfielders a keeper should be able to hit the ball with both feet. It's a great disadvantage if you're one footed. The opposition will soon find out and prey on the weakness. The standard ploy is usually to impede your stronger side and force you to use the less favoured foot.

There are two ways of kicking from your hands. First there's the drop kick or half volley. The purpose of this kick is to keep the ball on a low trajectory. You have to throw the ball up and make a firm contact as it hits the ground. When the ball is hit hard and low it gives the forwards more time to control than in the case of a heavenwards volley. One note of caution though, it is far easier to drop kick when the ground is firm, than when it's muddy. In heavy conditions it's hard to get the right accuracy or timing.

The second way of kicking from the hands is the volley. The fact that keepers have found the net at the other end from these kicks illustrates the power and distance you can get when you strike the ball correctly. You should spend time practising both the volley and the half volley until you're accurate enough to find your men. Many teams with a direct

91

style of play favour mighty upfield kicks from the keepers to get the ball into the opposing half.

When you're making a volley kick, decide on the player you're trying to 'hit', then keep your head down and eyes on the ball. Some goalies like to throw the ball high in the air before volleying,

You can achieve great power and distance if you strike the ball correctly

but that gives you a bigger chance of making an error. I prefer a small throw, almost placing the ball on my foot and hammering it as it drops. With good timing and a long follow through you can make the ball travel a long way into enemy territory.

When taking goal kicks, there are three main methods. First there's the long punt to the half-way line and

beyond for your forward players. Then there's the short kick to a colleague on the edge of the box, so you can collect a return pass for a volley kick. The third style is rarely used nowadays. That is a short chip over prowling forwards to a midfield player in space about 30 yards out. It can be very dangerous if this short chip or lob goes wrong. It's a kick which requires a lot of rehearsal.

I always like to see a goalkeeper use a variety of options when kicking. Whatever method you use, always look to find a man, rather than use a 'hoof and hope' kick.

Training

You could virtually write another book on this subject as there have been so many innovations in goalkeeper training over the years. The way goalies work out and sharpen their skills has altered radically over the last 20 years ... and most of the changes have been for the better.

Even when I started, goalkeepers used to do virtually the same training as outfield players. Now the idea of saving a few shots for the odd ten minutes a week has gone. In the Introduction I mentioned the sessions that many clubs have started on a regular basis to help their keepers. Training for a goalie has to be very specialised. When you're between the posts any faults will be exposed because you're in the most isolated place on the field. You must work in training on any weakness in your game. There are more skills in soccer for a goalie to develop than an outfield player.

As I've illustrated throughout this book, I'm always open to new ideas when studying the science of goalkeeping. I've mentioned how you can improve your play by examining other sports and looking at comparable actions and movements that may be of

benefit to your game. The fact that we've compared certain goalkeeping techniques with boxing, rugby, American football, swimming, fast bowling and even disco dancing shows how much can be learnt from other sports and activities.

Many different exercises and practice routines will help perfect your skills. Some are obvious. For shot stopping you can simply get team mates to fire in shots from all angles and distances. Try to select the two or three best strikers of the ball in your side for this workout. You can use a similar drill for catching and punching crosses. Get a few players to play the ball into the box from a variety of positions. To sharpen up your work you should get colleagues to challenge for the ball with you. Try to go for every cross with the determination you would show in a match. It's through this kind of practice that you'll be able to work out your positioning by trial and error.

You can work on the technique for coming off your line by inviting team mates to rush at you, then dive at their feet and wrench the ball away. Always remember these sort of situations will be harder in a match as you'll be up against foes rather than friends.

For goalkeepers, general fitness is as important as both quickness on the feet and agility. Even though I am at the veteran stage, I still have to keep my body flexible. Believe me, that's often as much a mental as physical effort!

Rhythm and strength are important. You have to be physically strong, with a reasonable physique, but not stiff and muscle bound. The muscles you need to strengthen are those in your arms, shoulders and stomach. You also need plenty of power in the legs to help your spring. A certain amount of weight training can be a help, but try to avoid static exercises – keep on the move. Don't bother lifting huge weights from a stationary position, that will only create excess bulk. Instead, use a circuit of exercises so you switch quickly from one discipline to another. It is the speed with which you carry out the exercises that is important.

Include some work to build up your wrists. It is important for a keeper to have wrists of equal strength.

Routines like the simple repetition of diving from one side to the other as described in the section on agility are excellent for combining work on speed and power.

To improve your reactions try a few simple foot movements. For example, jumping over balls and running from side to side and backwards as quickly as possible. Always use short, rather than long loping strides. Goalkeepers need many different qualities, but remember the three S's – Strength, Speed and Suppleness.

97

Captaincy

As I savoured every moment of leading my country in international football, you'd probably think that I advocate goalkeeper-captains. But I must confess that, as a general rule, I'm not in favour of the idea. Funnily enough, I think a keeper is quite capable of leading his country, but not an ideal choice to captain his club side.

I don't disagree with goalies taking charge of the team out on the field, I just feel it's a job that can be carried out better by an outfield player. Many goalies, though, have been successful captains. Gil Merrick, an England international in the fifties, skippered Birmingham City from between the posts. Mark Wallington had a spell as captain of one of my old clubs, Leicester City and Martin Hodge has led Sheffield Wednesday out onto the field. It always gives me a bit of encouragement to remember that Dino Zoff captained Italy to World Cup triumph in Spain in 1982 at the age of 40.

I've always enjoyed taking charge of England and I'm proud of my record as an international captain. I'd skippered England ten times before ending on the

Dino Zoff – captain of Italy's victorious 1982
World Cup team, aged 40

losing side, and that was against Argentina in the quarter-finals of the 1986 World Cup ... beaten by the hand and foot of Maradona!

It's from my experience with England that I've realised that, in many ways, it's easier for a goalkeeper to take charge of a national team than a club side. At international level the captaincy is often

99

Leading out England (here against Holland) is the greatest honour in the game

more of a prestigious appointment. The task isn't as hard as he's obviously surrounded by the country's most experienced and able players. There's an old adage in football that a good team has eleven captains on the field and in any national team there's usually two or three players who skipper their clubs.

Some people have come up with the theory that being in goal is an ideal position from which to direct operations. They argue that a keeper can see the whole match planned out in front of him. There's a certain amount of truth in that opinion, but an outfielder is in a better position to guide young players and pass on words of advice and encouragement during a game. For instance, it is very difficult for a keeper to have a word with his strikers during the heat of the battle.

As goalkeeping is such a specialised position that requires 100 per cent concentration, the worries of captaincy can be distracting. A goalie has to stay in charge of his territory and, as I've frequently mentioned, he's a team leader anyway ... in his own penalty area.

In many respects he has to be more selfish than an outfield player. Before the kick-off I like a very thorough warm up, not only to loosen the muscles, but also to test the wind direction, the surface of the pitch and other factors that affect goalkeeping. The duties of a captain ... helping to sort out team

102

problems, inspecting the pitch, tossing the coin and so forth can be a heavy burden to take on week in and week out.

Captaining England is the greatest honour I've experienced in over 20 years of football and I'd be thrilled to carry out the duty if I was asked again; but I'd prefer someone else to do the job at club level.

Kit

The marketing of football kit, and particularly goalkeeper's gear, has been a rapidly expanding business since I started in football. Anyone walking into a sports shop can be overwhelmed with the choice of goods on offer. You can buy boots and kit in every colour and design imaginable. Many products claim to have innovations that will help your game.

My advice is don't pay attention to the maker's name and design, but buy the gear that feels the most comfortable and suitable for *you*. It can often take weeks of saving up pocket money or generous contributions from parents to get funds to buy equipment. An important point to remember is that the most expensive articles aren't necessarily the best. So don't put pressure on your parents to get you the highest priced kit, it won't make you a better keeper. What is far more important is to see young players smartly turned out in their football strip. Never go on to the field in dirty boots and clothing. Clean and neat kit shows that a player has the right attitude.

Goalkeepers should always wear shin pads. I advise the type of pads that have

104

built-in ankle supports. I know some players like their socks rolled down, but that is a silly risk to take. Contrary to what some people think, modern pads don't restrict your movement in any way. At some time they'll save you from serious injury. One proviso I would make is for young keepers to dispense with the ankle supports in training as you need to strengthen the joints as much as possible.

Gloves are essential and an aspiring goalie needs two pairs. Modern technology has produced gloves for wet and dry weather. That's been a great advance in goalkeeping equipment as years ago the only choice was between bare hands and cumbersome string gauntlets. Always keep your spare pair of gloves in a watertight bag at the back of the goal. You can also use the bag to carry other useful articles like a spare pair of tie ups and a cap for that rare occasion when the sun is shining in your eyes.

Some goalies like to chew gum, but that is something I don't recommend. Gum can easily get stuck in your throat, which could be very dangerous. The main purpose of the gum is to keep your mouth moist. It's a far better idea to put a small carton of soft drink in your bag and have a quick sip if there's a long hold-up in play.

During training sessions it is advisable to wear padded jerseys, shorts or

Keeper's kit

tracksuit bottoms. This will prevent unnecessary cuts and bruises, especially when the ground is hard. When practising keeping, you'll be constantly diving around and any knocks you take will restrict your work and lead to injuries.

In matches you should only need to wear tracksuit bottoms for protection in three situations, on frost-bound ground, when the surface is bone hard and dry and on artificial pitches. Plastic or synthetic grass can cause unpleasant burns and abrasions if your legs are uncovered.

As with all items of kit there are many different types of jersey available. I have my own brand, but my advice is to find one with padded elbows and shoulders. Another useful piece of equipment is a good kit bag. Look for one large enough to hold all your playing and training gear.

Remember to take a pride in your appearance on the field ... if your kit is immaculate that will be reflected in your work. It doesn't cost a lot of money to ensure your clothing is clean and well ironed and your boots are polished.

107

Catching and
Smothering the Ball

Saving at Full Stretch

Throwing

Kicking from Hands